# CONTENTS

# INTRODUCTION

# FIRSTLY WHAT IS PHOTOGRAPHY?

PHOTOGRAPHY IS THE PRODUCT OF LIGHT REACTING WITH FILM OR YOUR DIGITAL SENSOR AS IT TRAVELS THROUGH YOUR LENS.
LIGHT ALSO SHAPES AND DETERMINES HOW WE SEE THINGS.

WHEN YOU UNDERSTAND HOW TO CONTROL THE LIGHT COMING THROUGH THE LENS OF YOUR CAMERA THEN YOU CAN START TO USE YOUR CAMERA MANUALLY AND MORE EFFECTIVELY TRANSLATE YOUR VISION INTO AN IMAGE.

ONCE YOU UNDERSTAND HOW TO EFFECTIVELY CAPTURE YOUR DESIRED IMAGE, THEN IT IS TIME TO REALLY DISCOVER WHAT YOU WANT TO COMMUNICATE THROUGH PHOTOGRAPHY.

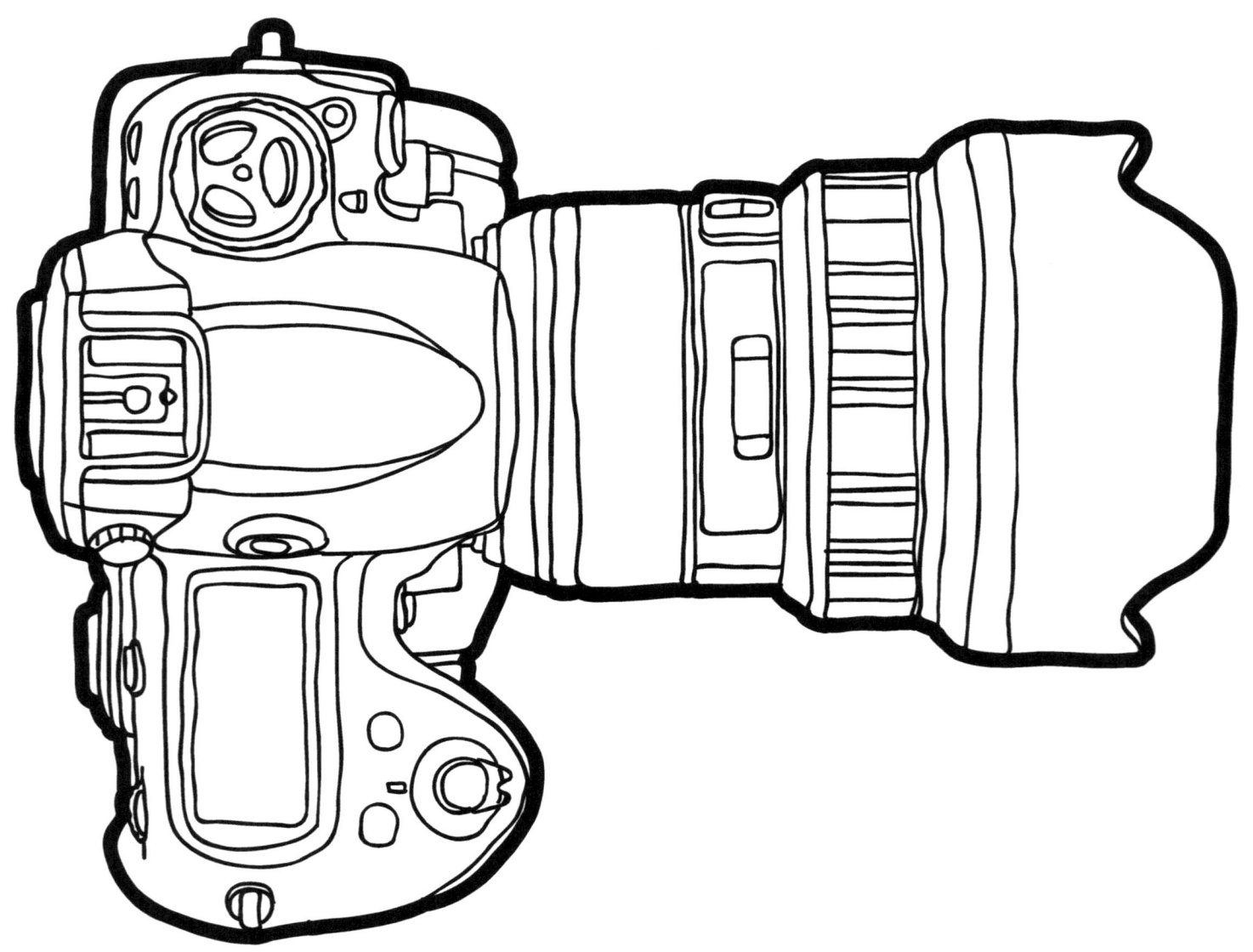

# THE PRINCIPLES OF PHOTOGRAPHY

HAVE NOT CHANGED OVER THE YEARS AND DIGITAL CAMERAS ALL WORK ON THE SAME PRINCIPLES AS FILM CAMERAS.

DIGITAL CAMERAS HAVE MADE PHOTOGRAPHY MORE IMMEDIATE AND GIVEN US GREATER FLEXIBILITY WHEN CREATING IMAGES.

## < LIGHT GOES IN THROUGH THE LENS

# PART 1
## GETTING STARTED

HOW TO SWITCH TO MANUAL EXPOSURE WITHOUT KNOWING ANYTHING TECHNICAL BEFORE YOU START.

N.B. HAVE YOUR CAMERA TO HAND. (IT MAY BE USEFUL TO ALSO HAVE YOUR CAMERA BOOKLET/MANUAL TO HAND). IT IS BEST TO TRY THIS OUTSIDE IN DAYLIGHT. THE INSTRUCTIONS GIVEN ARE GENERIC BECAUSE THE FUNCTIONS OF DIFFERENT BRANDS AND MODELS OF CAMERA DIFFER. IF IN DOUBT PLEASE CONSULT YOUR INSTRUCTION MANUAL.

THIS GUIDE IS FOR CAMERAS WITH A MANUAL OPTION. FIRSTLY CHOOSE THE MANUAL OPTION, WHICH MAY BE ON A DIAL OR DIGITAL DISPLAY - THIS WILL BE INDICATED BY THE LETTER "M".

NEXT, ADJUST YOUR ISO- AGAIN, THIS COULD BE ON A DIAL OR DIGITAL DISPLAY. CHOOSE ISO 200.

LOOK THROUGH THE VIEWFINDER TO LINE UP THE SCENE YOU WANT TO PHOTOGRAPH. ALONG THE BOTTOM EDGE OF YOUR VIEWFINDER YOU WILL SEE THE GRAPHIC BELOW, THIS WILL BE LIT.

THE AIM IS TO GET THE LIGHT TO ILLUMINATE IN THE MIDDLE OF THE PLUS AND MINUS. WHEN THIS HAPPENS YOU HAVE A CORRECT EXPOSURE.

TO ACHIEVE THIS YOU NEED TO CHANGE EITHER THE APERTURE OR THE SHUTTER SPEED, OR BOTH. THEY ARE USUALLY CHANGED BY MOVING THE DIALS OR BUTTONS ON TOP, OR ON THE BACK OF YOUR CAMERA.

YOU SHOULD HAVE ONE THAT OPERATES THE SHUTTER SPEED AND ONE THAT OPERATES THE APERTURE.

THE SHUTTER SPEED NUMBERS ARE MUCH LARGER THAN THE APERTURE SO IT WILL BE EASY TO IDENTIFY WHICH IS WHICH. THE NUMBERS WILL BE DISPLAYED THROUGH THE VIEWFINDER AND ALSO ON THE DIGITAL DISPLAY ON THE TOP OF THE CAMERA. TAKE YOUR TIME AND HAVE A PLAY WITH YOUR CAMERA UNTIL YOU FULLY UNDERSTAND THE INSTRUCTIONS SO FAR.

## APERTURE NUMBERS INCLUDE

## 2.8  4  5.6  8  11  16 22 32

### (AND ALL INCREMENTS IN BETWEEN)

## SHUTTER SPEED NUMBERS INCLUDE

## 30 60  125  250  500  1000  1500

## (AND ALL INCREMENTS IN BETWEEN AND EVEN HIGHER OR LOWER)

# NOW, A FEW SIMPLE RULES —

LOOK AT YOUR PROPOSED SCENE: YOU NEED TO BE CAREFUL WHERE THE EXPOSURE COMES FROM. IDEALLY, YOU WANT TO LOOK FOR A NEUTRAL AREA THAT IS WITHIN YOUR SCENE. BY NEUTRAL I MEAN NOT FACING INTO THE SUN AND NOT IN THE SHADOWS - SOMETHING THAT REPRESENTS THE LIGHT OF THE SCENE, BUT NOT THE EXTREMES LIKE SHADOW OR BRIGHT SUN.

# FOR EXAMPLE -

IF YOU WANT TO PHOTOGRAPH A LANDSCAPE, POINT YOUR CAMERA TOWARDS THE GROUND TO MAKE THE NECESSARY ADJUSTMENTS THEN RE-FRAME THE SHOT USING THAT EXPOSURE. DO NOT WORRY IF THE INDICATOR MOVES TOWARDS THE PLUS, THIS WILL BE RESPONDING TO THE SUNLIGHT. TRUST IN THE PROCESS. TAKE THE SHOT AND VIEW THE IMAGE. IF IT LOOKS TOO DARK, RETAKE THE EXPOSURE, ALLOWING THE INDICATOR TO GO SLIGHTLY TOWARDS THE PLUS. IF IT IS TOO LIGHT RETAKE THE EXPOSURE ALLOWING THE INDICATOR TO GO SLIGHTLY TOWARDS THE MINUS. KEEP DOING THIS UNTIL THE IMAGE LOOKS RIGHT TO YOU.

PRACTICE IS THE ONLY WAY TO GET THIS RIGHT. DO NOT CONCERN YOURSELF WITH ANYTHING ELSE UNTIL YOU UNDERSTAND THIS PROCESS.

WHEN I FIRST STARTED LEARNING PHOTOGRAPHY THIS IS EXACTLY HOW I WAS TAUGHT. I WAS TOLD NOTHING ELSE. JUST HOW TO GET AN EXPOSURE IN THE WAY I HAVE DESCRIBED ABOVE.

THE ONLY OTHER PIECE OF ADVICE WAS TO PHOTOGRAPH SOMETHING THAT INTERESTED ME.

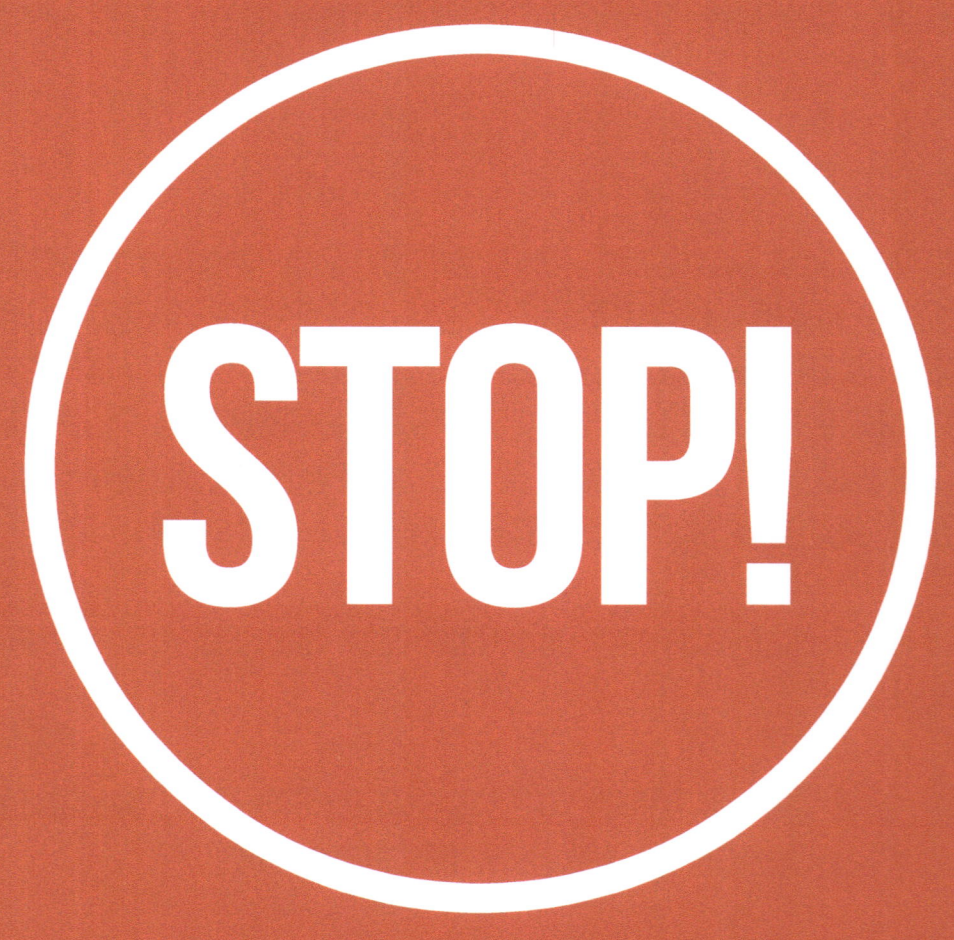

# HAVE YOU PRACTISED PART 1?

## ARE YOU COMFORTABLE CHANGING SETTINGS ON YOUR CAMERA?

## IF NOT, GO BACK!

# ARE YOU SURE YOU ARE READY FOR THE NEXT STEP?

# PART 2
## LESSON 1

### EXPOSURE

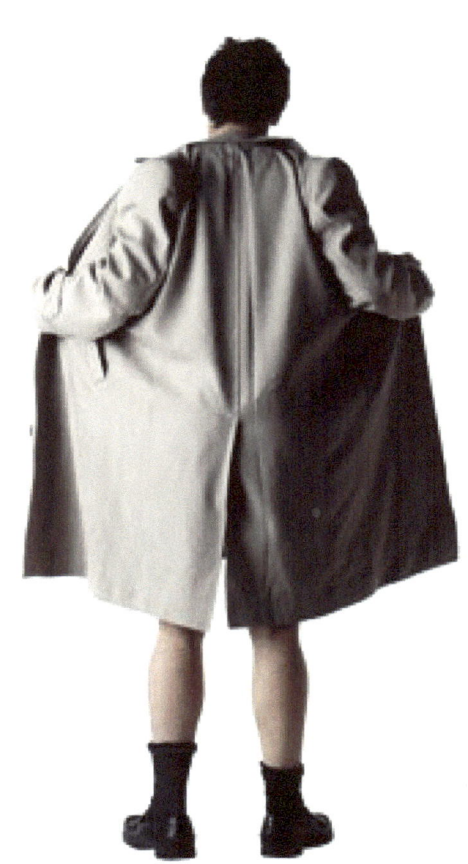

# THERE ARE THREE KEYS TO MANUAL EXPOSURE. FIRST, YOU NEED TO UNDERSTAND EACH KEY INDIVIDUALLY AND THEN HOW THEY WORK IN TANDEM WITH ONE ANOTHER.

## THE 3 KEYS ARE —

### SHUTTER SPEED -

THIS RELATES TO THE MOVEABLE COVER THAT ALLOWS LIGHT ONTO YOUR CAMERA SENSOR OR FILM IN THE BODY OF THE CAMERA.

### APERTURE, F/STOPS -

THIS RELATES TO HOW MUCH LIGHT IS ALLOWED THROUGH THE LENS OF YOUR CAMERA.

### ISO/ ASA/ FILM SPEED -

THIS RELATES TO THE EXTERNAL CONDITIONS AND AVAILABLE LIGHT, E.G. A SUNNY DAY, CLOUDY DAY, LOW LIGHT (NIGHT OR INDOORS).

EACH ONE OF THESE KEYS PLAYS AN IMPORTANT PART IN THE DIFFERENT ASPECTS OF THE EXPOSURE, IN DETERMINING HOW YOUR IMAGE WILL LOOK AND FEEL. THE CHOICES YOU MAKE WITH EACH OF THE KEYS AND HOW YOU PRIORITISE THEM IS ALSO IMPORTANT.

# LESSON 2

APERTURE

THINK OF A LENS AS AN ADJUSTABLE TUBE THAT DECREASES OR INCREASES IN DIAMETER DEPENDING ON THE SETTING (F STOP). IF YOU WERE TO LOOK INTO YOUR LENS WHILE CHANGING THE SETTINGS, THIS CHANGE WOULD BE VERY EASY TO SEE.

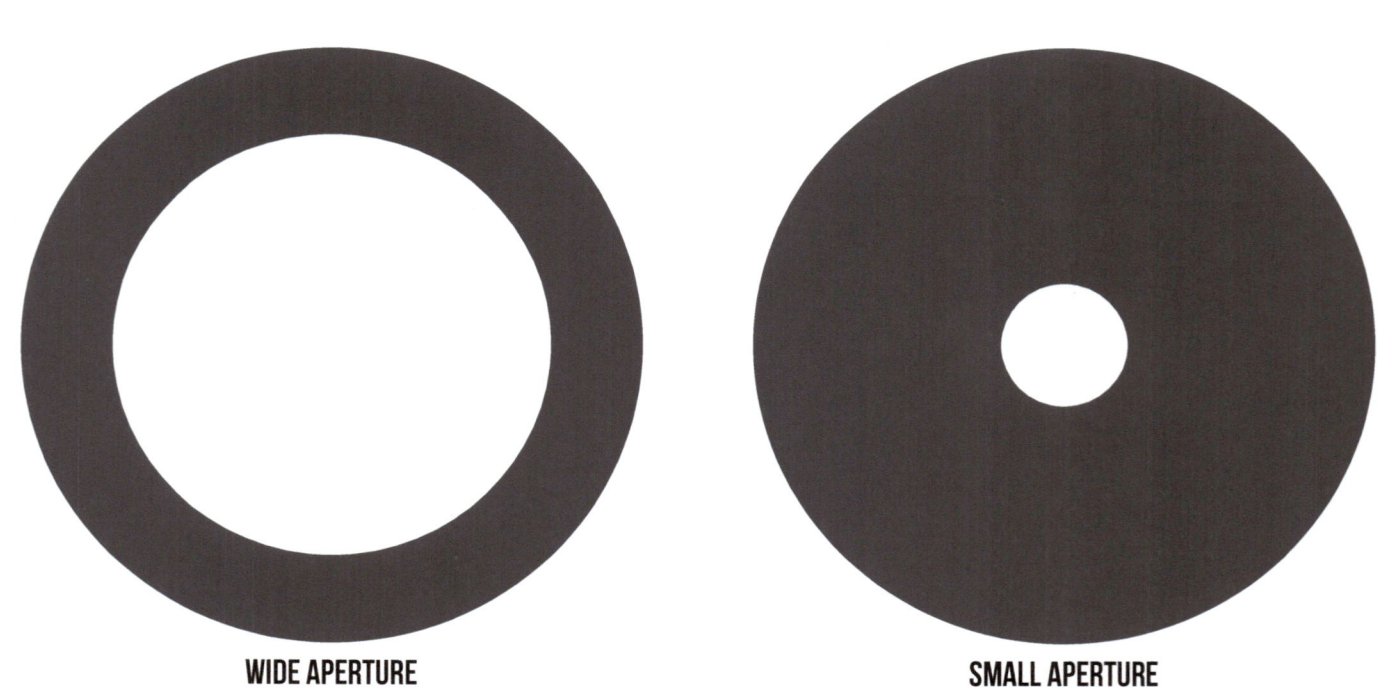

WIDE APERTURE

SMALL APERTURE

ON OLD FILM CAMERAS THE APERTURE INCREMENTS WERE CLEARLY MARKED ON THE BARREL OF THE LENS. E.G.

## 2.8 4 5.6 8 11 16 22 32

THESE INCREMENTS ARE CALLED F STOPS. THE DIFFERENCE BETWEEN EACH INCREMENT IS ONE STOP. THEY ARE ALL OF EQUAL VALUE TO EACH OTHER. FOR EXAMPLE, TO CHANGE FROM F4 TO F5.6 WOULD HAVE THE SAME IMPACT AS ON THE EXPOSURE AS A CHANGE FROM F8 TO F11.

## THE WIDER THE APERTURE, THE MORE LIGHT IS ALLOWED THROUGH THE LENS; THE SMALLER THE APERTURE, THE LESS LIGHT IS ALLOWED THROUGH.

HENCE, F2.8 IS THE WIDEST APERTURE AND F32 IS THE SMALLEST.

THE SAME RULES APPLY ON A DIGITAL CAMERA. A DIGITAL CAMERA WILL ENABLE YOU SET THE APERTURE IN SMALLER INCREMENTS THAN THOSE DESCRIBED. IF YOU DO THIS THEN YOU WILL BE DIVIDING THE F STOP INTO A FRACTION. YOU MAY NOTICE THAT NOT ALL LENSES HAVE THE SAME CAPABILITY OR RANGE OF F STOPS , SOME MAY RANGE FROM F4 TO F22.

# THERE IS A SIMPLE PHRASE THAT WILL HELP YOU REMEMBER -

# THE BIGGER THE NUMBER THE SMALLER THE HOLE.

F32                       F2.8

# LESSON 3

SHUTTER SPEEDS

IN A DIGITAL CAMERA, THE SENSOR IS IN THE BODY OF THE CAMERA WHERE THE FILM WOULD ORIGINALLY HAVE BEEN. THE SHUTTER COVERS THE SENSOR/FILM. WHEN YOU PRESS THE CAMERA TRIGGER THE SHUTTER IS RELEASED, EXPOSING THE SENSOR/FILM. THE SPEED OF THE SHUTTER DETERMINES THE LENGTH OF TIME YOU EXPOSE THE SENSOR.

# IF YOU WANT MORE LIGHT ONTO THE SENSOR, USE A SLOW SHUTTER SPEED.

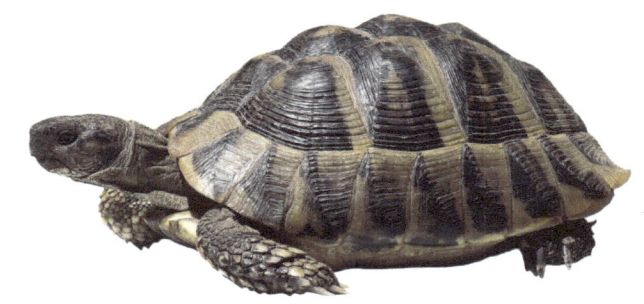

# IF YOU WANT LESS LIGHT ONTO THE SENSOR, USE A FAST SHUTTER SPEED.

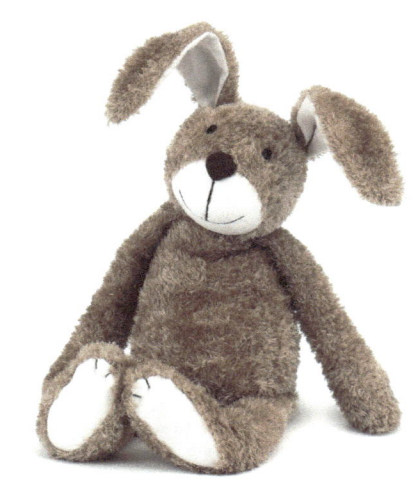

ON AN OLD FILM CAMERA THESE WOULD HAVE BEEN CLEARLY MARKED, FOR EXAMPLE —

# 8TH   15TH   30TH   60TH   125TH   250TH   500TH   1000TH

THEY ARE ALL FRACTIONS OF A SECOND.

AS WITH THE APERTURE, EACH ONE IS OF EQUAL VALUE TO THE OTHER AND THE ABOVE NUMBERS ARE SE-QUENCED IN STOPS. THE DIFFERENCE BETWEEN EACH INCREMENT IS ONE STOP (AS WITH APERTURE).

SHUTTER SPEED AFFECTS THE WAY MOVEMENT IS CAPTURED: IF YOU WANT TO FREEZE MOTION YOU NEED A HIGH SHUTTER SPEED, IF YOU WANT TO BLUR MOTION YOU NEED A LOW SHUTTER SPEED.

# ALL SPEEDS ARE RELATIVE TO THE SPEED OF THE MOVEMENT

E.G. A MOVING CAR WILL BE FASTER THAN A MAN WALKING.

N.B.
A SHUTTER SPEED LOWER THAN A 60TH WILL REQUIRE A TRIPOD OR YOU RISK CAMERA SHAKE.

# LESSON 4

## ISO / ASA

# UNDERSTANDING ISO/ ASA / FILM SPEED

ISO, ASA AND FILM SPEED ARE ALL ONE IN THE SAME, THEY'RE JUST DIFFERENT TERMINOLOGY.
BEFORE DIGITAL CAMERAS WERE AROUND YOU WOULD HAVE TO CHOOSE A FILM THAT WAS APPROPRIATE FOR
THE LIGHTING CONDITIONS.

# NOW WE HAVE THAT CHOICE WITHIN THE CAMERA, GIVING YOU FAR GREATER FLEXIBILITY AT YOUR FINGERTIPS.

HOWEVER, BE AWARE THE HIGHER THE ISO THE MORE NOISE WILL BE CREATED. NOISE IS THE DIGITAL EQUIVALENT TO GRAIN WHEN USING FILM. IT COULD BE DESCRIBED AS VERY SMALL DOTS THAT ARE APPARENT IN THE IMAGE.

N.B.

AS TECHNOLOGY IMPROVES SO DOES THE QUALITY OF LOW LIGHT PHOTOGRAPHY. IF YOU HAVE RECENTLY PURCHASED A NEW MODEL OF CAMERA YOU MAY FIND WHEN YOU USE A HIGH ISO THE QUALITY IS VASTLY IMPROVED AND NOISE IS REDUCED IN COMPARISON TO OLDER MODELS.

# HOW TO CHOOSE THE CORRECT ISO —

100 ISO FOR A BRIGHT SUNNY DAY

200 ISO FOR A CLOUDY BRIGHT DAY

400 ISO FOR A CLOUDY GREY DAY

800 ISO IN LOW LIGHT, DUSK OR INSIDE

1600 OR HIGHER ISO DARK CONDITIONS

AGAIN, THESE EACH HAVE AN EQUAL VALUE TO EACH OTHER AND ARE NUMBERED IN STOPS.

YOUR CAMERA WILL ALLOW YOU TO CHOOSE INTERMITTENT NUMBERS. IF YOU CHOOSE AN ISO IN BETWEEN THESE NUMBERS THEN THEY WOULD BE A FRACTION OF A STOP.

# LESSON 5

## CAMERA SETTINGS

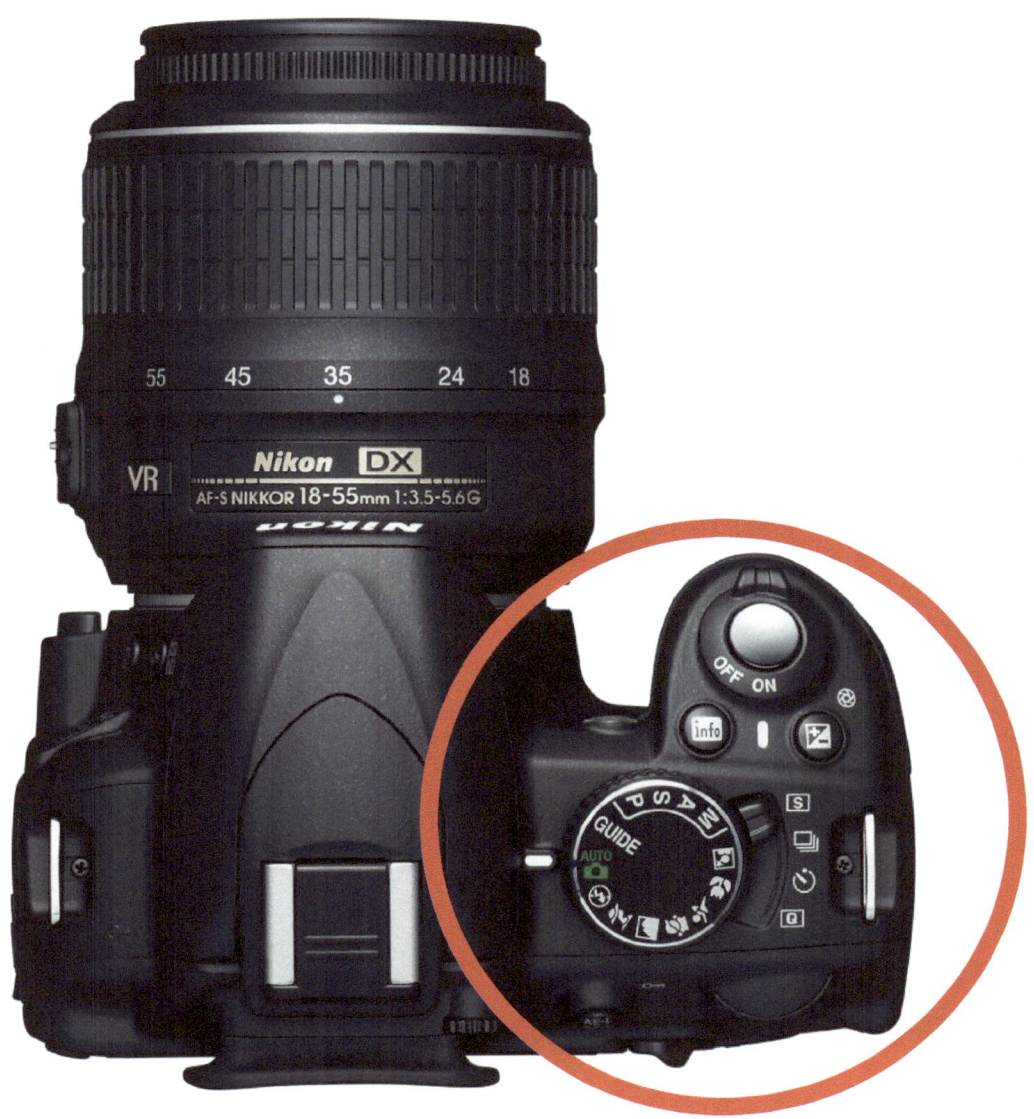

# UNDERSTANDING CAMERA SETTINGS

ALL CAMERAS HAVE A SELECTION OF SETTINGS TO ULTIMATELY GIVE YOU CHOICE AND DIFFERENT LEVELS OF AUTO MATION.

## AUTO
FULLY AUTOMATIC

## PROGRAM
YOU CAN CHOOSE THE ISO AND THE CAMERA CHOOSES EVERYTHING ELSE

## APERTURE PRIORITY
YOU CHOOSE THE APERTURE AND THE CAMERA SETS THE SHUTTER SPEED

## SHUTTER SPEED PRIORITY
YOU CHOOSE THE SHUTTER SPEED AND THE CAMERA SETS THE APERTURE

## MANUAL
YOU ARE ON YOUR OWN

## BULB
THIS ALLOWS YOU TO OPEN THE SHUTTER FOR AS LONG AS YOU WANT. (YOU NEED A CABLE RELEASE AND TRIPOD USE THIS SETTING)

DEPENDING ON YOUR LEVEL OF EXPERTISE AND SPEED OF USE, CHOOSE THE APPROPRIATE SETTING FOR YOUR SPECIFIC SUBJECT. THESE SETTINGS WILL GIVE A SLIGHTLY DIFFERENT LOOK TO THE IMAGE THAN USING THE AUTOMATIC MODE.

YOUR CAMERA MAY ALSO HAVE OTHER SETTINGS E.G. LANDSCAPE, PORTRAITURE, ETC.; THESE MAKE GENERAL CHOICES ON YOUR BEHALF, APPROPRIATE TO YOUR CHOSEN SUBJECT.

FOR EXAMPLE:

# PORTRAITURE
THIS WILL CREATE A SHALLOW DEPTH OF FIELD. ( I WILL DESCRIBE DEPTH OF FIELD LATER)

# LANDSCAPE
THIS WILL GIVE YOU GOOD DEPTH OF FIELD.

# NIGHT MODE
WILL CHOOSE A HIGH ISO

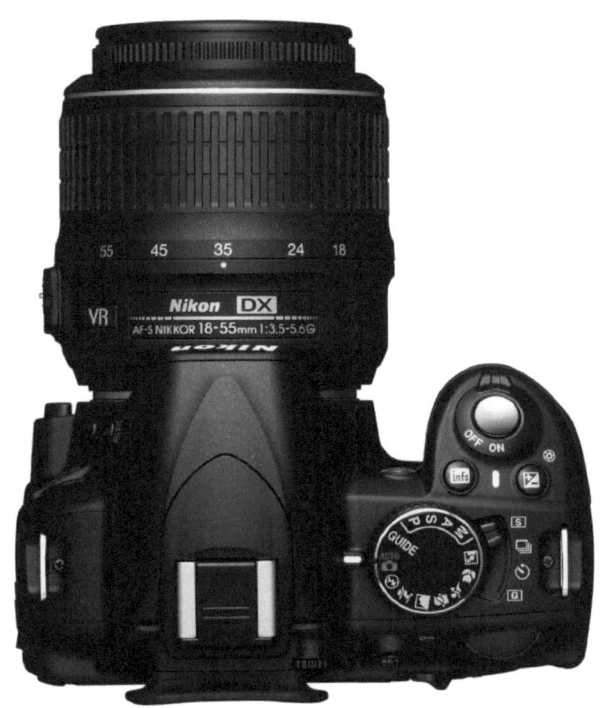

# LESSON 6

## DEPTH OF FIELD

# UNDERSTANDING DEPTH OF FIELD

YOU DETERMINE THE DEPTH OF FIELD BY THE APERTURE YOU CHOOSE. REMEMBER I TOLD YOU ABOUT APERTURE AND HOW IF THE APERTURE IS WIDE OPEN IT ALLOWS A LOT OF LIGHT THROUGH THE LENS? WELL, SIMILARLY, THE WIDER THE APERTURE, THE LESS DEPTH OF FIELD AND THE SMALLER THE APERTURE, THE MORE DEPTH OF FIELD. AN IMAGE WITH A PERSON SHARP IN THE FOREGROUND, BUT THE BACKGROUND IS VERY SOFT WITH LITTLE VISIBLE DETAIL, THAT WOULD BE DESCRIBED AS SHALLOW DEPTH OF FIELD.

FOR AN EXAMPLE OF THIS, SEE THE NEXT PAGE.

THIS BEE AND THISTLE IMAGE PERFECTLY ILLUSTRATES SHALLOW DEPTH OF FIELD.

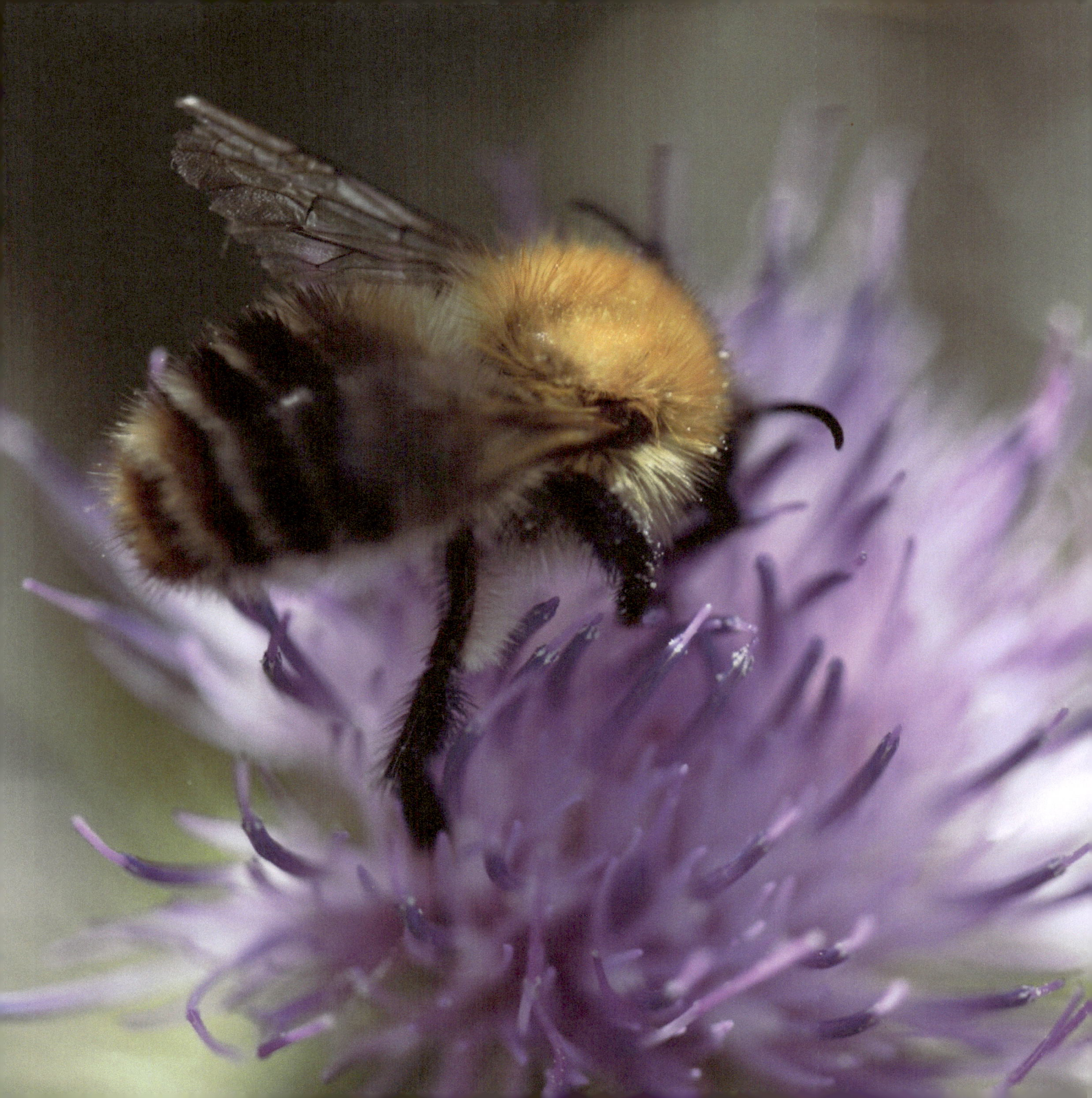

THE OTHER END OF THE SPECTRUM WOULD BE A LANDSCAPE WHERE THERE IS LOTS OF FINE DETAIL AND EVERY THING LOOKS VERY SHARP. THIS WOULD BE DESCRIBED AS HAVING GOOD DEPTH OF FIELD.

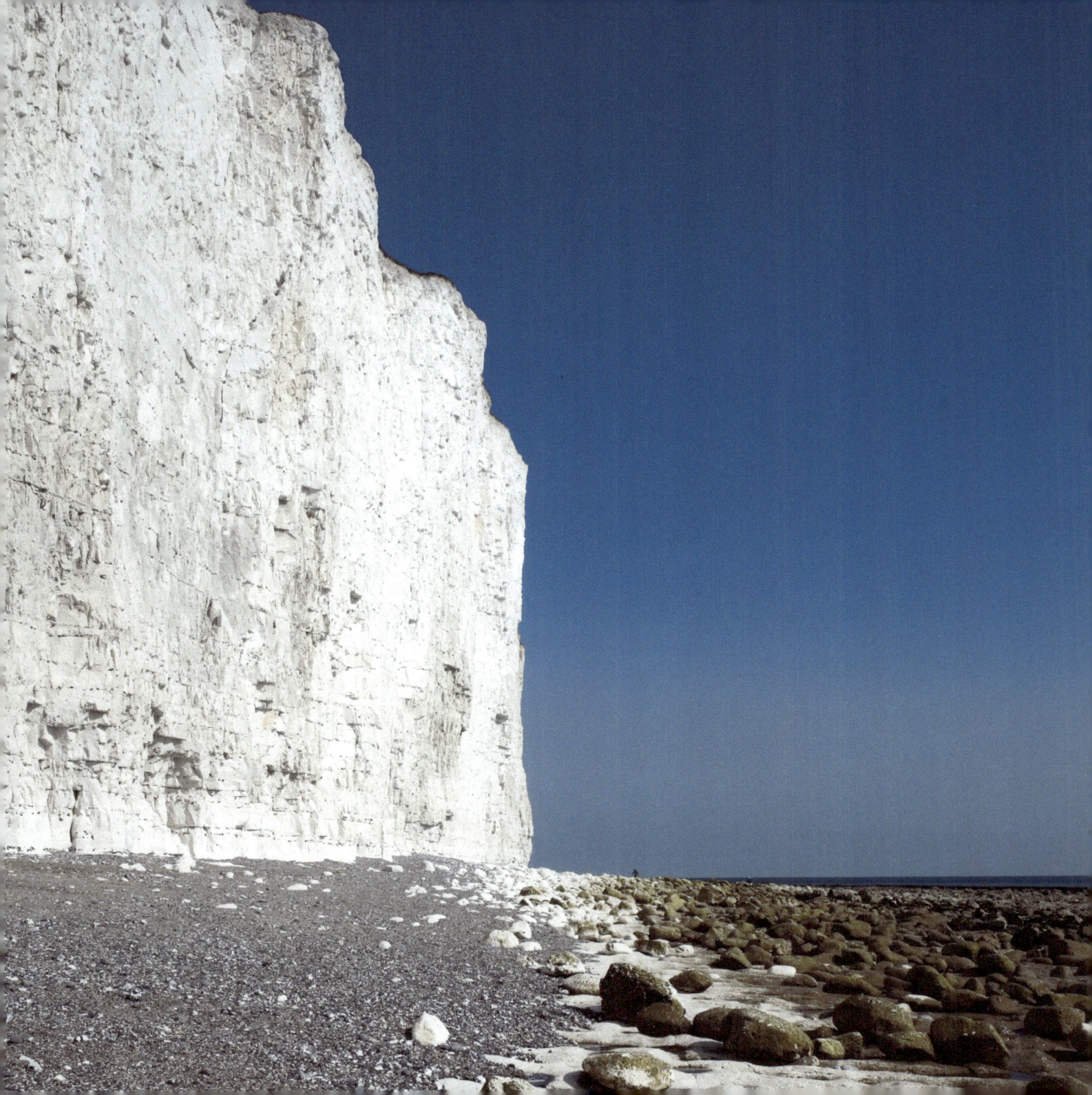

# LESSON 7

## UNDERSTANDING THE DIFFERENCE BETWEEN SHOOTING BLACK + WHITE AND COLOUR

# UNDERSTANDING THE DIFFERENCE BETWEEN SHOOTING BLACK + WHITE AND COLOUR.

DIGITAL HAS GIVEN US SO MUCH FLEXIBILITY AND THAT INCLUDES BEING ABLE TO SWAP BETWEEN BLACK + WHITE AND COLOUR IMAGERY AT THE TOUCH OF A BUTTON. HOWEVER, NOT ALL COLOUR IMAGES WILL TRANSLATE WELL INTO BLACK + WHITE. ONLY WHEN YOU FULLY UNDERSTAND WHAT CREATES A GOOD COLOUR OR BLACK + WHITE IMAGE WILL YOUR PHOTOGRAPHS IMPROVE.

## WHAT MAKES A GOOD COLOUR IMAGE?

COLOURS GIVE OFF VIBRATIONS, SO IF YOU USE COLOUR IN A COMPLIMENTARY WAY THEN THE COLOUR ENHANCES THE SUBJECT MATTER. FOR EXAMPLE, IF YOU HAVE A RED ROSE SURROUNDED BY BRIGHT GREEN FOLIAGE, THE COLOURS VIBRATE WITH EACH OTHER AND ADD ANOTHER DIMENSION TO THE IMAGE. THINKING ABOUT COLOUR AS A SUBJECT MATTER RATHER THAN THE OBJECT CAN HELP DEVELOP A BETTER UNDERSTANDING OF HOW COLOUR CAN BE USED TO ENHANCE YOUR IMAGES.

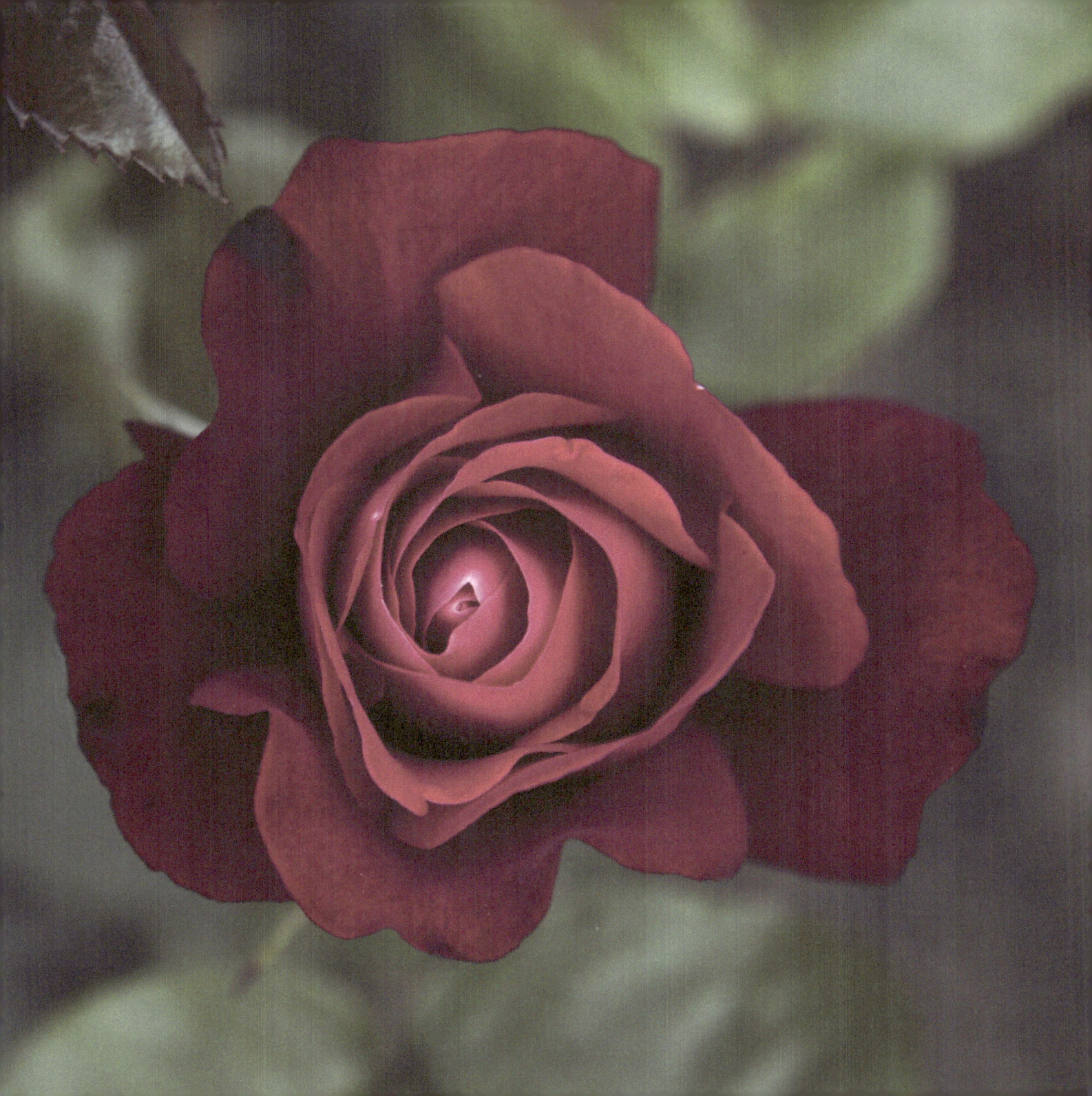

# WHAT MAKES A GOOD BLACK + WHITE IMAGE?

CONTRAST OR LACK THEREOF, IS THE KEY HERE. BLACK + WHITE IS ALL ABOUT TONALITY AND HOW YOU CREATE DIFFERENCE WITH TONE OR SUBTLETY OF TONE. AT ONE END OF THE TONAL SCALE YOU HAVE THE HIGHLIGHT AND AT THE OPPOSITE END YOU HAVE BLACK WITH VARIOUS SHADES OF GREY IN BETWEEN.

THE AIM OF CREATING A GOOD BLACK + WHITE PHOTOGRAPH IS TO CAPTURE AS MANY DIFFERENT TONES AS POSSIBLE, WHILST STILL HAVING TEXTURE IN BOTH THE HIGHLIGHTS AND BLACKS.

A GOOD WAY IS TO THINK OF YOUR SUBJECT AS BLACK + WHITE INSTEAD OF COLOUR. IF WE TAKE THE PREVIOUS EXAMPLE OF THE RED ROSE AND GREEN FOLIAGE, AND CONVERT IT TO A BLACK + WHITE IMAGE. RED AND GREEN HAVE THE SAME TONAL VALUE, SO APPEAR AS SIMILAR GREYS. THUS THE IMPACT THE COLOUR HAD IS LOST.

THE IMAGE OF THE BLACK + WHITE ROSE ON THE NEXT PAGE ILLUSTRATES THIS.

HOWEVER, IF THE RED ROSE WAS WHITE THE CONTRAST BETWEEN THAT AND THE MID GREY OF THE FOLIAGE WOULD WORK WELL AS A BLACK + WHITE IMAGE.

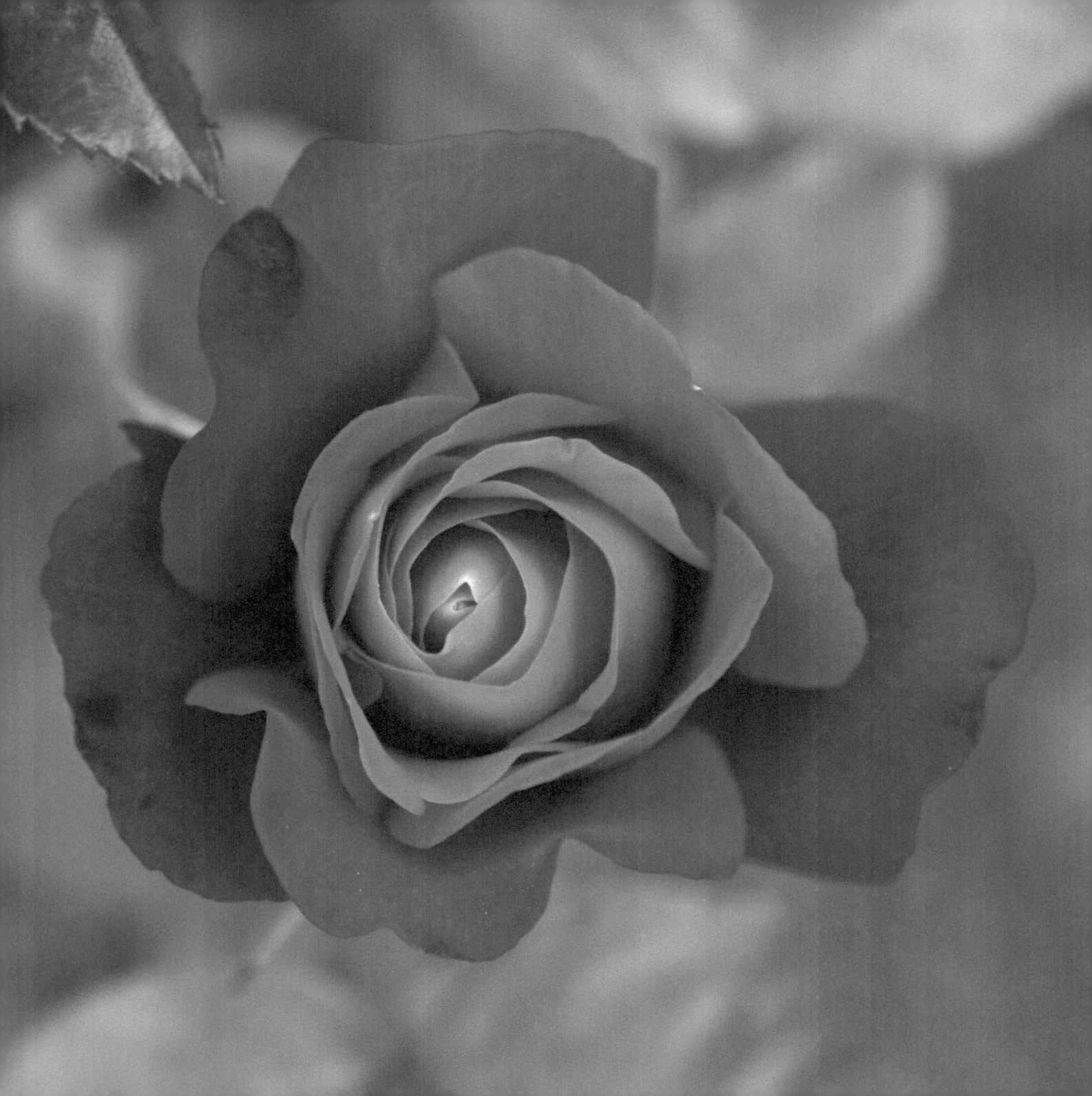

SUBTLETY OF TONE ALSO WORKS WELL IF THE IMAGE IS MADE UP OF VERY LIGHT TONES. SEE THE EXAMPLE IMAGE OF THE SEASCAPE ON THE NEXT PAGE.

# LESSON 8

## METERING READINGS

# UNDERSTANDING METERING READINGS.

YOUR CAMERA HAS A BUILT IN LIGHT METER THAT TAKES A REFLECTIVE LIGHT READING OFF WHATEVER YOU POINT IT AT. LIGHT BOUNCES OFF THE OBJECT INTO THE CAMERA AND THE CAMERA WILL INDICATE WHETHER YOU HAVE THE CORRECT AMOUNT OF LIGHT, TOO MUCH LIGHT OR NOT ENOUGH LIGHT.

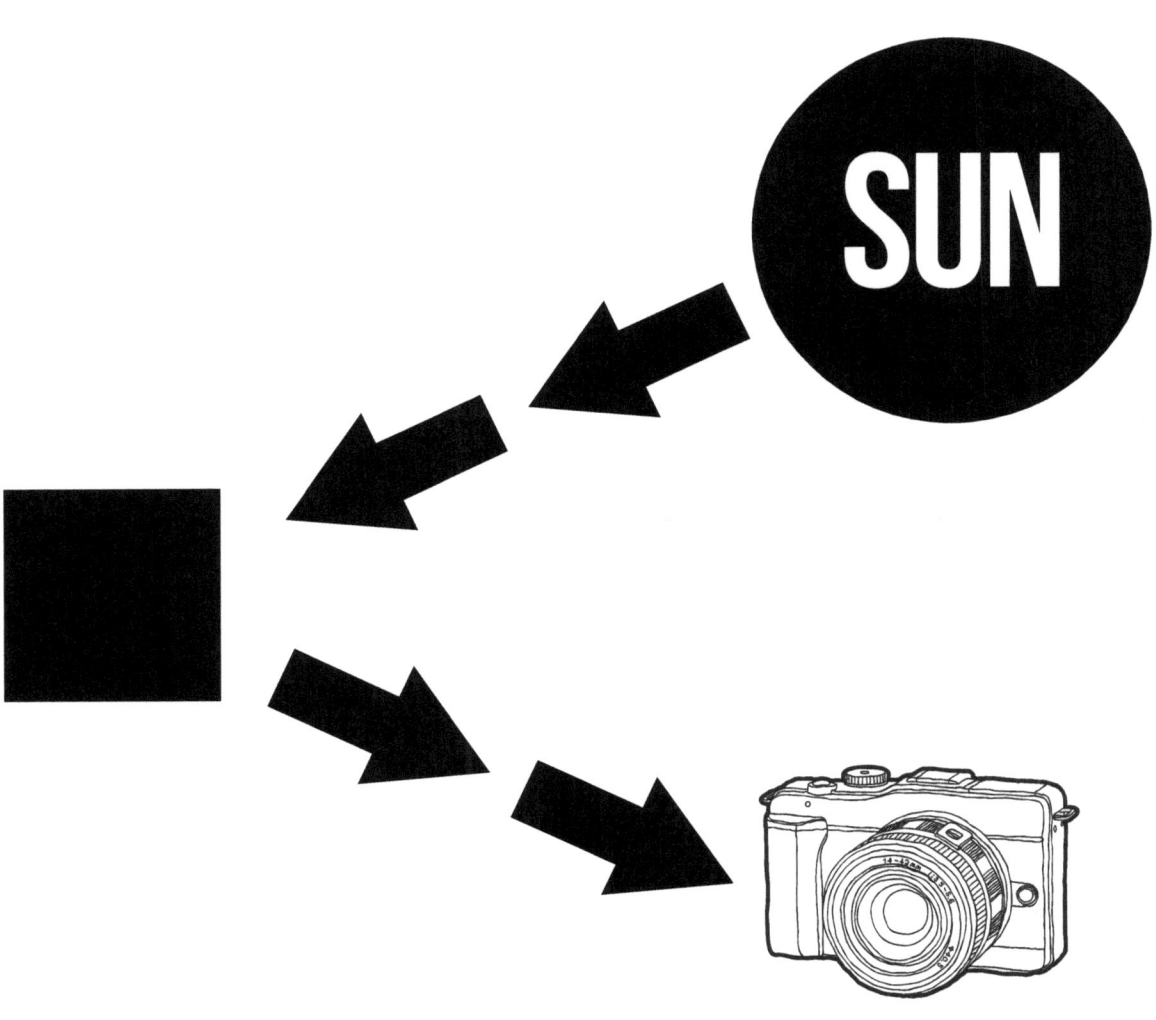

YOU THEN NEED TO ALTER EITHER THE SHUTTER SPEED, THE APERTURE OR BOTH, UNTIL YOUR CAMERA INDICATES THE CORRECT AMOUNT OF LIGHT.
THIS USUALLY DISPLAYS THUS —

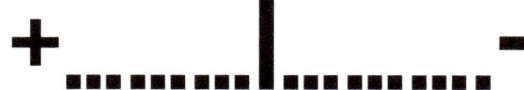

WHEN THE INDICATOR IS DIRECTLY IN THE MIDDLE OF THE + AND - THEN THE EXPOSURE IS CORRECT.

**TOO MUCH LIGHT** — YOU NEED TO COMPENSATE BY EITHER CLOSING THE APERTURE (CHANGING TO A HIGHER NUMBER) OR CHANGING TO A FASTER SHUTTER SPEED.

**NOT ENOUGH LIGHT** — YOU NEED TO COMPENSATE BY EITHER OPENING THE APERTURE (CHANGING TO A LOWER NUMBER) OR CHANGING TO A LOWER SHUTTER SPEED.

THE ISO SHOULD ONLY BE CHANGED AS A LAST RESORT, IF CHANGING THE APERTURE AND THE SHUTTER SPEED DO NOT GIVE YOU ENOUGH OPTIONS. IF YOU WANT MORE LIGHT, USE A HIGHER ISO AND FOR LESS LIGHT, USE A LOWER ISO.

IF YOU REMEMBER, IN PREVIOUS LESSONS I DESCRIBED THAT EACH OF THE 3 KEYS ARE MEASURED IN STOPS. THIS ALLOWS YOU TO CHANGE A CORRECT EXPOSURE TO A DIFFERENT EXPOSURE THAT IS ALSO CORRECT BUT ALLOWS FOR MOVEMENT OR DEPTH OF FIELD.

# FOR EXAMPLE - YOU HAVE A CORRECT EXPOSURE OF -100 ISO 125TH OF A SECOND SHUTTER SPEED AND F11 APERTURE

REFER TO THE TEXT BELOW TO HELP YOU CALCULATE EXPOSURE CHANGES

## SHUTTER SPEEDS
8TH   15TH   30TH   60TH   125TH   250TH   500TH   1000TH

## F-STOPS
2.8   4   5.6   8   11   16   22   32

THE AIM IS TO HAVE A VERY SHALLOW DEPTH OF FIELD, SO YOU NEED A VERY WIDE APERTURE OF F4.

IF YOUR STARTING EXPOSURE IS 100 ISO 125TH OF A SECOND SHUTTER SPEED AND F11 APERTURE, WE NEED TO COMPENSATE 3 STOPS WITH OUR APERTURE TO F4. BECAUSE WE HAVE ADDED 3 STOPS TO OF LIGHT WITH OUR APERTURE, WE NEED TO COMPENSATE WITH THE SHUTTER SPEED BY 3 STOPS TO ALLOW LESS LIGHT.

OUR EXPOSURE IS NOW 100 ISO 1000TH OF A SECOND AT APERTURE F4

# EXAMPLE - IF WE WANT TO CHANGE THE SHUTTER SPEED TO FREEZE THE MOVEMENT OF A MOVING CAR, WE MAY WANT TO USE 1000TH OF A SECOND

F4 IS A SHALLOW DEPTH OF FIELD AND WE WOULD LIKE MORE DEPTH OF FIELD (MORE BACKGROUND DETAIL), BUT WE NEED THE SHUTTER SPEED TO STAY AT 1000TH OF A SECOND TO FREEZE A CAR'S MOVEMENT. IF WE CHANGE THE APERTURE BY 2 STOPS TO F8 TO ALLOW MORE DEPTH OF FIELD, THEN TO COMPENSATE WE NEED TO CHANGE THE ISO TO 400.

# THE ABOVE DESCRIPTION IS A GOOD EXAMPLE OF HOW TO USE THE ISO TO CREATE A DIFFERENT EXPOSURE.

ALL THIS TAKES A LOT OF PRACTISE AND PATIENCE, BUT IN TIME IT WILL BECOME SECOND NATURE AND YOU WILL QUICKLY FIND YOURSELF MAKING THE RIGHT DECISION AT THE RIGHT TIME.

# QUIZ

## A

IF YOU HAVE A CORRECT EXPOSURE OF 100 ISO, F8 AT 60TH, BUT YOU WANT VERY SHALLOW DEPTH OF FIELD, HOW WOULD YOU CHANGE THE EXPOSURE ?

## B

IF YOU HAVE A CORRECT EXPOSURE OF 200 ISO, F8 AT 250TH, BUT YOU WANT TO PHOTOGRAPH A MOVING CAR AND BLUR THE MOTION, HOW WOULD YOU CHANGE THE EXPOSURE?

ANSWERS
A - 100 ISO, F4 AT 250TH
B - 200 ISO, F16 AT 60TH

# LESSON 9

## HOW TO SELECT THE CORRECT METERING MODE

# HOW TO SELECT THE CORRECT METERING MODE

YOUR CAMERA MAY HAVE DIFFERENT METERING OPTIONS, (CHECK YOUR MANUAL), INCLUDING –

## EVALUATIVE –
THE CAMERA TAKES IN ALL THE INFORMATION FROM THE LIGHTING CONDITIONS IN THE WHOLE OF THE SCENE AND EVALUATES THE CORRECT EXPOSURE.

## PARTIAL –
THIS IS MORE USEFUL WHEN THE BACKGROUND IS MUCH BRIGHTER THAN THE SUBJECT IN THE FOREGROUND AND TAKES MORE INFORMATION FROM THE CENTRAL AREA OF THE VIEW FINDER.

## SPOT –
THIS TAKES A READING FROM THE CENTRE SPOT IN YOUR VIEW FINDER AND IS GOOD AT EVALUATING A READING FOR A SPECIFIC AREA OF YOUR SCENE, FOR EXAMPLE A PERSONS FACE.

## CENTRE –
WEIGHTED AVERAGE METERING – THIS TAKES A READING FROM THE CENTRAL AREA, THEN AVERAGES THAT READING FOR THE WHOLE OF THE SCENE.

IF YOU ARE USING YOUR CAMERA MANUALLY I WOULD SUGGEST USING SPOT METERING, AS THIS ALLOWS YOU TO TAKE A READING FROM A SPECIFIC AREA OF YOUR SCENE, GIVING YOU MORE CONTROL OVER THE EXPOSURE.

REMEMBER HOW I EXPLAINED HOW YOUR CAMERA TAKES A REFLECTIVE METER READING? LIGHT BOUNCES OFF THE OBJECT AND INTO THE LENS. IF YOU CHOOSE SPOT METERING YOU CAN ACCURATELY METER THE LIGHT BOUNCING OFF AN OBJECT. REMEMBER, A DARK OBJECT WILL ABSORB LIGHT AND A LIGHT OBJECT WILL REFLECT LIGHT.

# HOW TO GET A CORRECT EXPOSURE

**FIRSTLY CHOOSE YOUR ISO** BASED ON THE LIGHTING CONDITIONS. EXAMPLE - IF IT IS A BRIGHT SUNNY DAY CHOOSE 100 ISO. REFER TO PREVIOUS LESSON FOR GUIDELINES.

THEN THINK ABOUT YOUR SUBJECT: IS YOUR SUBJECT MOVING? IF IT IS THEN YOUR NEXT CONSIDERATION SHOULD BE THE SHUTTER SPEED. DO YOU WANT BLUR (SLOW SHUTTER SPEED) OR TO FREEZE THE SUBJECT IN MOTION (FAST SHUTTER SPEED).

NB. YOUR METER READING WILL DEPEND ON THE TONALITY OF YOUR SUBJECT. IF YOU TAKE A READING OFF A DARK OBJECT IT WILL BE LESS REFLECTIVE THAN A LIGHT OBJECT. IN THE SAME LIGHTING CONDITIONS YOU COULD GET DIFFERENT METER READINGS OFF DIFFERENT SURFACES.

TIP: WHEN TAKING A LIGHT READING WITH YOUR CAMERA NEVER POINT IT INTO THE SUN OR DARK SHADOW. YOU NEED TO TAKE THE READING FROM A MID-GREY TONE, FOR EXAMPLE GRASS, MID-GREY CONCRETE, THE PALM OF YOUR HAND. YOU THEN USE THIS EXPOSURE BUT RE-FRAME YOUR IMAGE.

THIS MAY SEEM CONFUSING TO BEGIN WITH, BUT TRUST IN THE PROCESS IT WILL WORK.

# LESSON 10

# WHAT TO PHOTOGRAPH?

IT'S A GOOD THING TO START WITH A SUBJECT YOU ARE PASSIONATE ABOUT - FAMILY, FRIENDS, PETS, A FAVOURITE PLACE, A HOBBY.

PHOTOGRAPHY IS A FORM OF COMMUNICATION. WHAT DO YOU WANT TO COMMUNICATE TO YOUR AUDIENCE?

AMAZING IMAGES DO NOT HAPPEN BY ACCIDENT. THE PHOTOGRAPHER HAS AN AGENDA IN MIND, AN INTENTION. THE STRONGER THE INTENTION THE MORE POWERFUL THE IMAGE WILL BE.

## FOR EXAMPLE

IF YOU GO FOR A WALK ALONG A RIVER YOUR SENSES ARE ASSAULTED BY SIGHTS, SOUNDS, COLOURS AND SMELLS. YOU MAY FEEL OVERWHELMED BY THE AMOUNT OF THINGS TO PHOTOGRAPH. IF YOU TRIED TO CONVEY THE EXPERIENCE IN A COUPLE OF IMAGES IT CAN SEEM A DAUNTING TASK. BUT, IF YOU TAKE ONE ELEMENT OF YOUR WALK - SAY, THE REFLECTIONS OF THE RIVERBANK IN THE WATER - AND FOCUS YOUR ATTENTION ON THIS ONE SUBJECT, YOU WILL EXPLORE THIS ONE ELEMENT IN MORE DETAIL AND SHOW A MORE DEFINED POINT OF VIEW. THE PHOTOGRAPHS YOU PRODUCE WILL SHOW MORE OF AN INTENTION AND DRAW ATTENTION TO AN ASPECT OF THE RIVER THAT WE ARE ALL AWARE OF, BUT DO NOT LOOK AT SO CLOSELY.

## WHAT WOULD YOU LIKE TO FOCUS YOUR ATTENTION ON?

PHOTOGRAPHS ARE A REFLECTION OF THE PHOTOGRAPHER, THEIR POINT OF VIEW OF THE WORLD THEY SEE.

## AS A PHOTOGRAPHER WHAT WILL YOUR IMAGES SAY ABOUT YOU?

# SUMMARY

# SUMMARY

WHEN YOU BUY A CAMERA FAMILIARISE YOURSELF WITH IT'S FUNCTIONS (USE THE MANUAL). START TO USE IT EVEN IF IT IS JUST IN AUTOMATIC MODE. IF YOU FEEL OVERWHELMED, TRY THE DIFFERENT SETTINGS ONE AT A TIME .

GET COMFORTABLE WITH EACH SETTING, THEN TRY A NEW ONE. PRACTISE, PRACTISE, PRACTISE IS THE KEY TO GREAT PHOTOGRAPHY!

# THIS IS JUST THE BEGINNING!
# TO BE CONTINUED.......

IT WOULD BE ADVISABLE TO GET A NOTE BOOK TO RECORD THINGS LIKE EXPOSURES WHEN TRYING OUT YOUR MANUAL SKILLS, NOTES ON THINGS THAT HAVE OR HAVEN'T WORKED, IDEAS FOR THINGS TO PHOTOGRAPH OR JUST DOODLING!

TURN THE PAGE FOR IMAGE IDEAS

INSPIRATION IS ALL AROUND YOU! YOU JUST HAVE TO LOOK!
PETS AND FAMILY MAKE GOOD SUBJECTS, MEET MY CAT OLIVER ON THE NEXT PAGE:

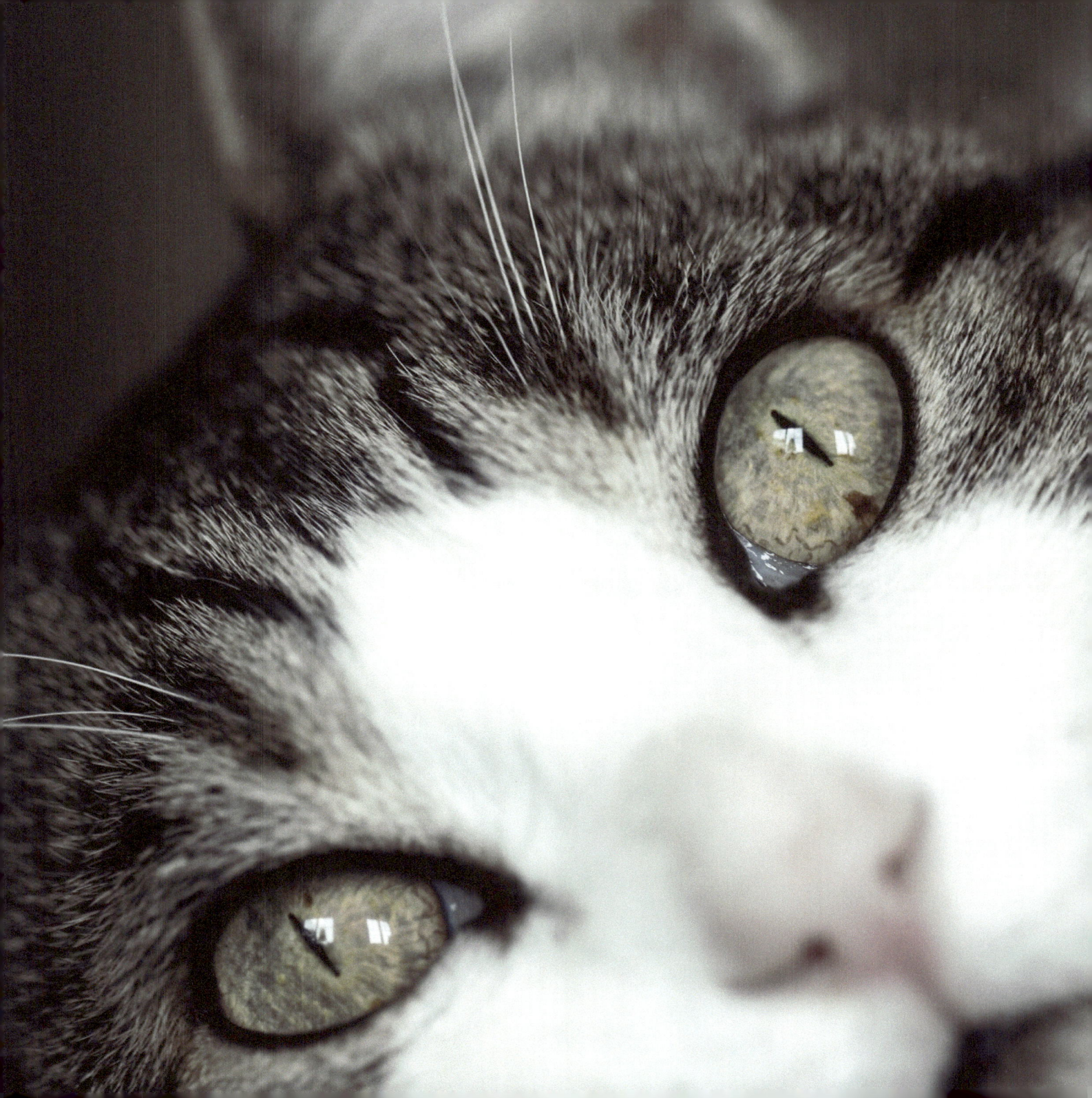

THE IMAGE OPPOSITE IS EASTBOURNE PIER, WEST SUSSEX, UK.
IT WAS ONE OF THOSE AMAZING DAYS WHEN THE SKY IS CHARCOAL AND THE SUN
IS BRIGHT. CHANGES TO THE AVAILABLE LIGHT CAN MAKE A HUGE DIFFERENCE TO
YOUR IMAGES.

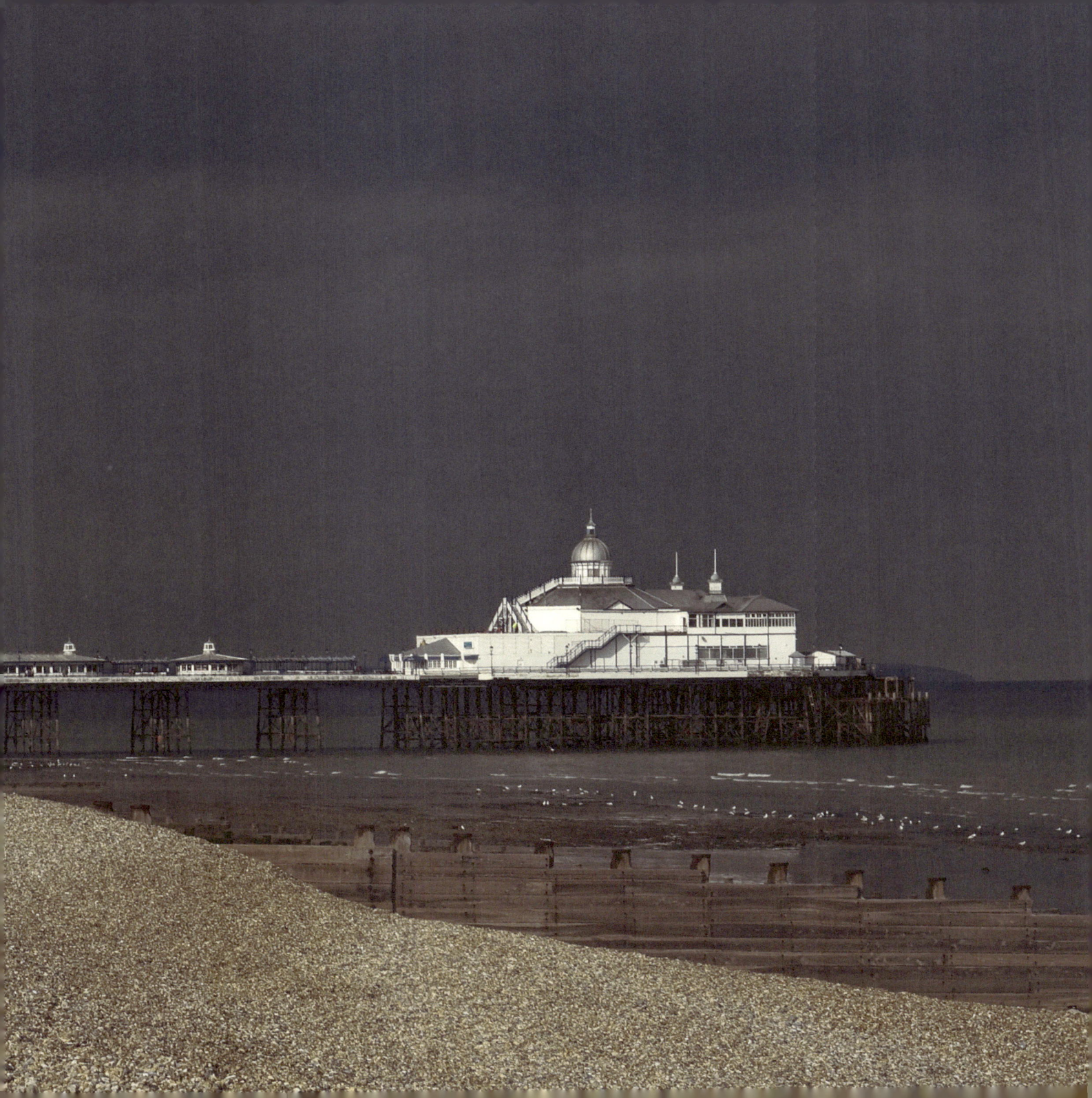

CONEY ISLAND, NEW YORK, USA - PEOPLE WAITING AT A PEDESTRIAN CROSSING. WHAT IS RIGHT IN FRONT OF YOU?

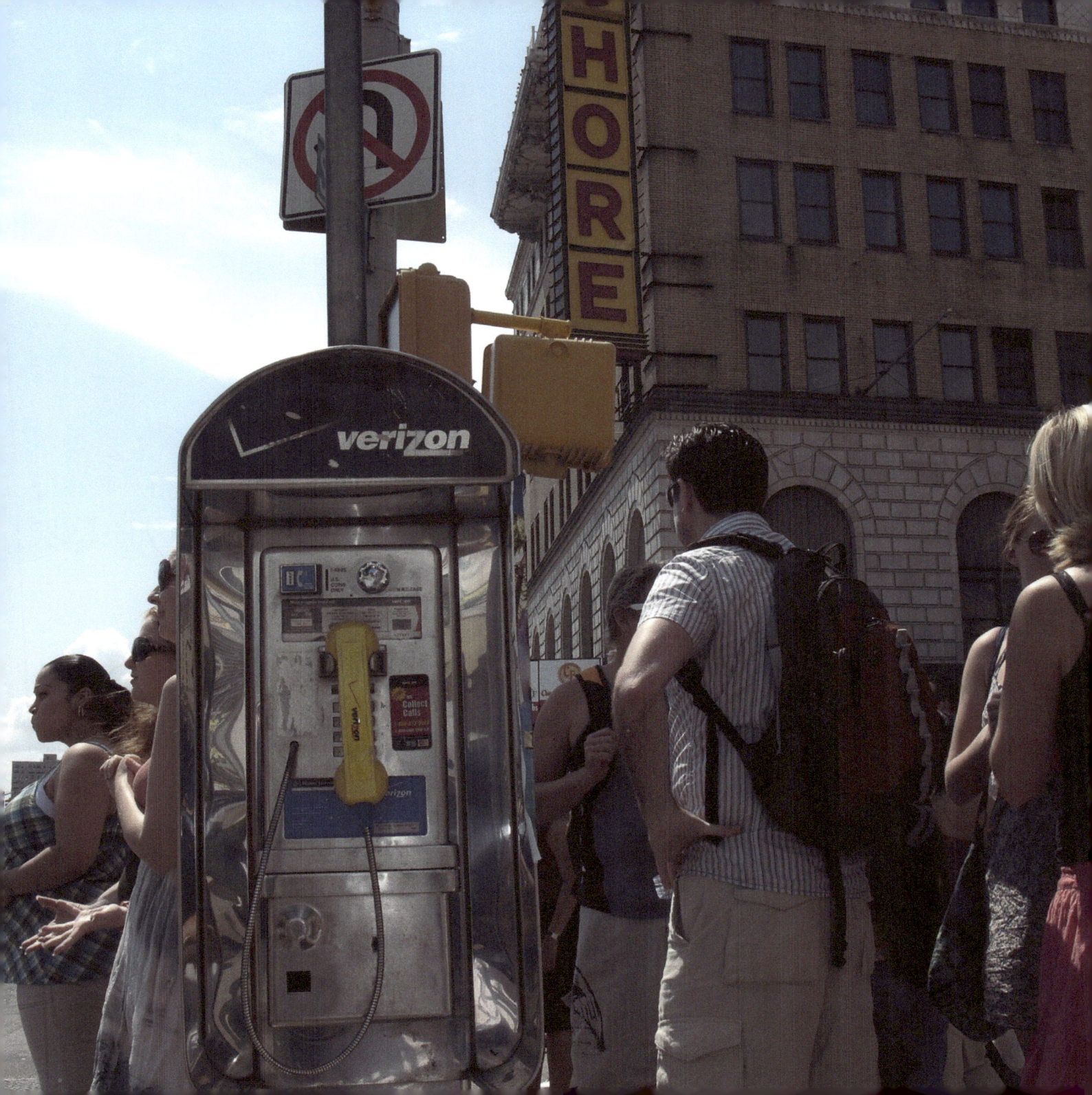

A NEW BORN MONKEY HOLDING ON TO HER MOTHER AT LONDON ZOO. CHANCE ENCOUNTERS ARE GREAT, TAKE ADVANTAGE OF OPPORTUNITIES THAT ARISE, BE FLEXIBLE!

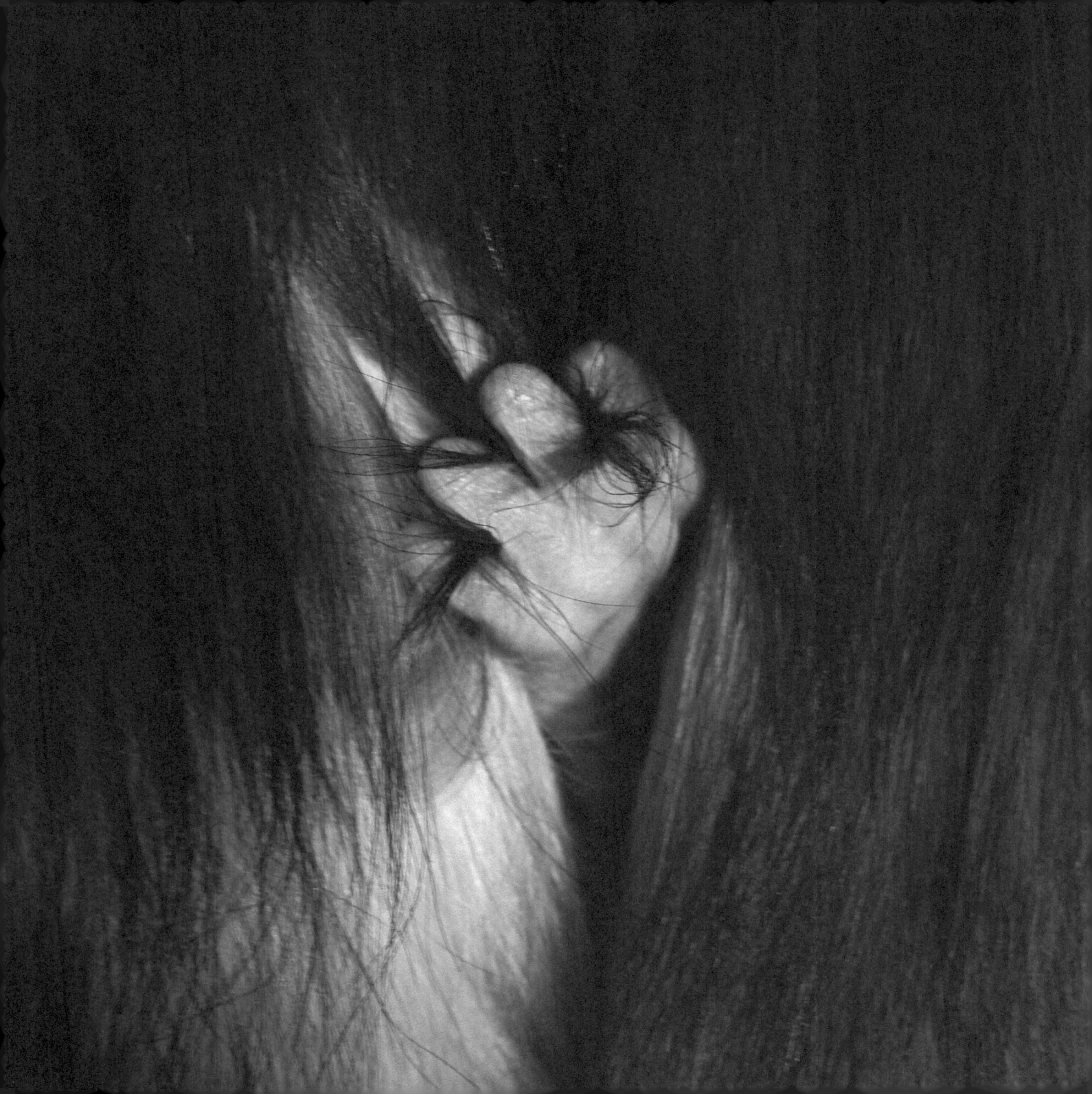

ST PAUL'S CATHEDRAL, LONDON, UK, AT NIGHT.
THINK ABOUT WHEN IS A GOOD TIME TO TAKE PHOTOGRAPHS.

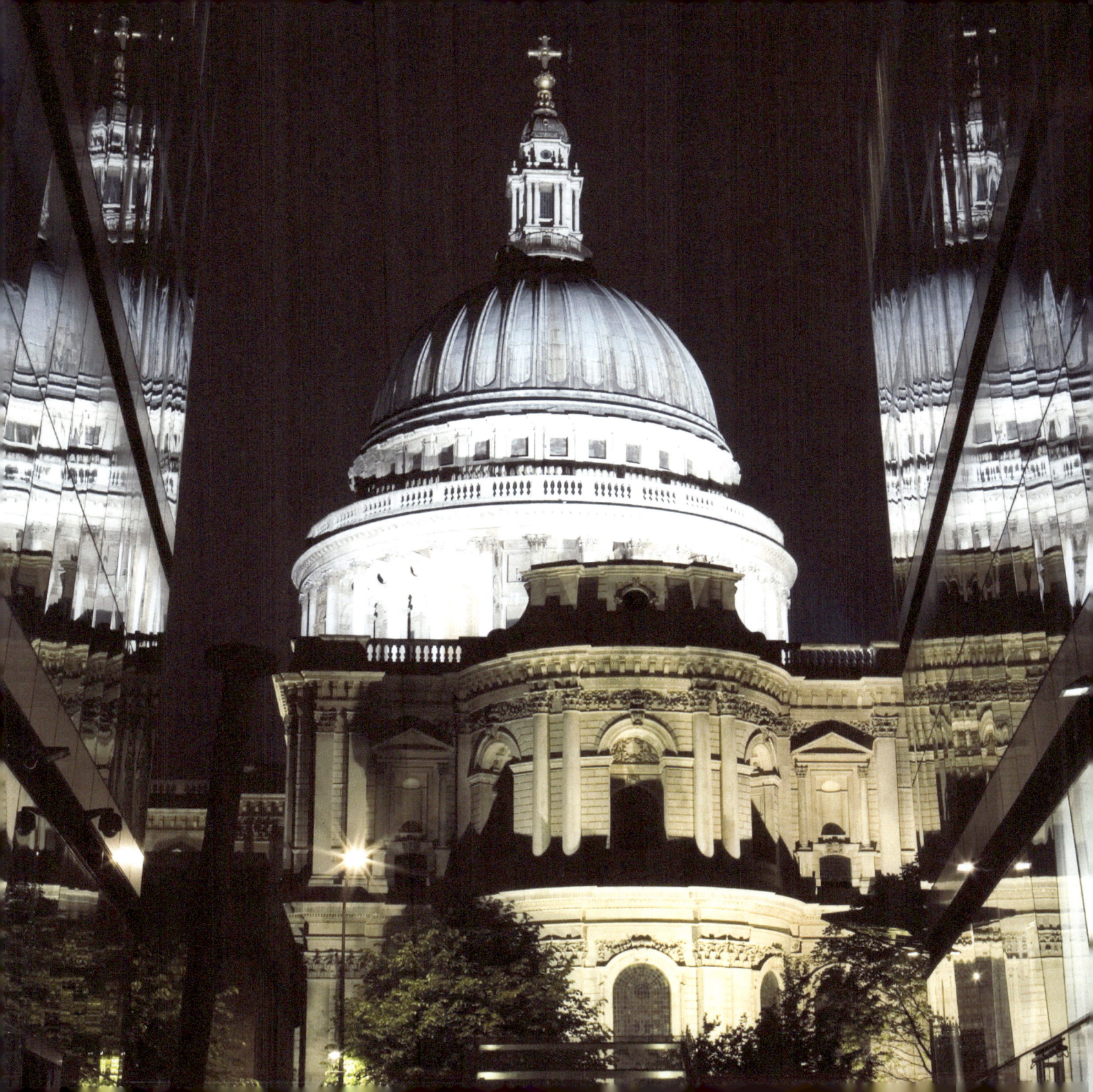

# ABOUT THE AUTHOR

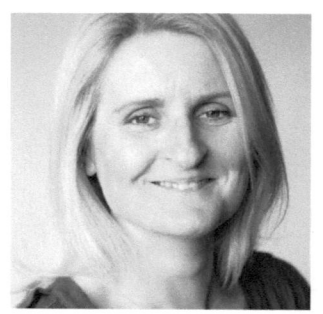

TEENA TAYLOR IS A DEGREE TRAINED PROFESSIONAL PHOTOGRAPHER AND HAS WORKED COMMERCIALLY SINCE THE MID 1990S, NATIONALLY AND INTERNATIONALLY WITHIN EDITORIAL, DESIGN AND ADVERTISING .

TEENA ALSO PRODUCES SELF INITIATED, LONG-TERM PROJECTS THAT GIVE HER THE OPPORTUNITY TO EXPLORE HER INTERESTS IN PEOPLE, SOCIETY AND CULTURE. SHE LIVES ON THE EDGE OF SOUTH WEST LONDON, IN SURREY.

CLIENTS HAVE INCLUDED - THE BRITISH HEART FOUNDATION, THE TRAINING AND DEVELOPMENT AGENCY, THE ROYAL BRITISH LEGION, MS SOCIETY, WEIGHT WATCHERS, ORION PUBLISHING, PENGUIN PUBLISHING, SATURDAY TIMES, MAIL ON SUNDAY YOU MAGAZINE, SUNDAY INDEPENDENT REVIEW, SATURDAY INDEPENDENT MAGAZINE, THE GUARDIAN WEEKEND, OBSERVER, MANAGEMENT TODAY, EASY LIVING, PSYCHOLOGIES, GRAZIA, BORSEN, MAMM, INTERMEDIAR, COTE OUEST, JOHN BROWN PUBLISHING, COUNTRY LIFE, RARE PUBLISHING, THUMBNAIL GUIDES.

COMMENDATIONS IN THE CATAGORIES OF; FINE ART, ABSTRACT, NATURE, PORTRAIT, BOOK, WILDLIFE, TAYLOR'S PICTURES HAVE BEEN COMMENDED IN -

THE PHOTOGRAPHIC MASTERS CUP INTERNATIONAL COLOUR AWARDS (2010)

THE BLACK AND WHITE 5TH ANNUAL SPIDER AWARDS (2009)

THE PX3 PRIX DE LA PHOTOGRAPHIE PARIS INTERNATIONAL COMPETITION (2007)

IPA LUCIE AWARDS (2005,2006) EXHIBITIONS

THE INTERNATIONAL FOTOGRAPHIA FESTIVAL AT HADRIAN'S TEMPLE, ROME, ITALY (2006)


EXHIBITIONS -

NATIONAL PORTRAIT GALLERY TAYLOR WESSING EXHIBITION 2015, LONDON, ENGLAND

THE INTERNATIONAL FOTOGRAPHIA FESTIVAL AT HADRIAN'S TEMPLE, ROME, ITALY (2006). THE MALL GALLERIES, THE MALL, LONDON, ENGLAND (1990).

VIEWPOINT PHOTOGRAPHY GALLERY, MANCHESTER, ENGLAND (1987).

INAUGURAL EXHIBITION AT VIEWPOINT PHOTOGRAPHY GALLERY , MANCHESTER, ENGLAND (1986).

# COME AND JOIN ME

I HOPE YOU HAVE FOUND THIS BOOK VALUABLE. IF YOU WOULD LIKE TO KNOW MORE PLEASE VISIT....

# WWW.SWITCHTOMANUALPHOTOGRAPHY.COM

# HAPPY SHOOTING!!!

www.ingramcontent.com/pod-product-compliance
Lightning Source LLC
Chambersburg PA
CBHW041314180526
45172CB00004B/1093